More FOR EAGLE EYES

Written and illustrated by Rolf Heimann

Watermill Press

First published in USA by Watermill Press.

First published by Periscope Press, a division of Roland Harvey Studios,
Australia.

Printed in USA

ISBN 0 8167 2614 0
10 9 8 7 6 5 4 3 2 1

In this book you will find 13 picture puzzles that will test your skill as an armchair detective. Read the story, then try to solve the mystery. And when you arrive at the solutions, you will find that they ask more questions than they answer! So, close the bedroom door, sharpen up your eagle eyes and attempt to conquer the mysteries that lie ahead. Good luck!

Angus and Vinny were expert divers, but even expert divers can get careless when they are excited. And finding the wreck of an old sailing ship had certainly been exciting. Angus was about to explore the dark inside of the wreck when he felt something pulling on his leg. At first he feared that a shark had grabbed him and he was relieved to see it was only a rope. But the more he struggled to free himself, the tighter the rope wrapped itself around his legs. This was serious! Fortunately Angus and Vinny always dived together so that they could help each other when one of them got into trouble. Angus gestured to his friend to get his knife and cut the rope.

But where was Vinny's knife? Vinny too had panicked and had dropped it.

Help Vinny to find his knife.
It can't be far.

Jessie and Hannah were pleased that Sir Pfifferstone had invited them along on a little expedition. They had never seen a forest like that! "Yes, it's totally unexplored country," explained Sir Pfifferstone proudly. "I've heard reports of a large beetle that looks like a leaf and a butterfly that resembles pink snakeweed. If you are the first to discover them, I shall name them after you."

"Why is it called pink *snakeweed?*" asked Hannah, nervously glancing around.

"Because it's pink, silly girl!" laughed Sir Pfifferstone. "And by the way, keep an eye out for snakes, they're deadly around here..."

It took the girls only two minutes to discover the beetle and the butterfly. If you are quicker, you can name them after yourself!

3

"Stop right there!" called McRob, the notorious crown thief. "I warn you, sir, this is my latest fiendish invention —the 'House of Security.' Observe please: if you dare to cut the strings, the balloons will rise, burst on the sharp nails above, thus waking my cat, Ginger, who will jump off. The weight will then drop into the tank making the water overflow and setting in motion the devilish mechanism that will plunge you into my patented mixture of crocodiles, snakes and scorpions. So take heed, sir!"

The king's musketeer hesitated for a moment, then laughed, "You underestimate my speed, you scoundrel. But even if I were as slow as a snail I would not fear your silly machine. It will not work as you say. To prove it I will cut the strings and stay right here on the trap door!"

Would you be just as confident?

"I don't know much about art," said the king, "but I know what I like. I like my pictures to be lifelike. I just spent a lot of money on my new castle and the least I expect from you chaps is that you can get the number of windows and the number of towers right. Whoever can do that will marry my daughter here, the lovely Princess Rebecca."

The painters took one good look at Princess Rebecca and decided to make a deliberate mistake so that they wouldn't have to marry her. Only one of the painters was so dedicated to his art that he couldn't bring himself to paint anything incorrectly.

Which one was it?

S. Carlett

It had been fun riding the old steam train to Eaglestone. Now Anton and Antonia meant to catch the 2:30 P.M. train to Lakeside. "I am sorry," apologized the conductor, "but the train to Lakeside is an hour late." "Oh no," exclaimed Anton. "Our friends will be waiting for us. We told them that our train would arrive there at 3:00 P.M. Is there a way that we can get to Lakeside earlier?"

"Well," mused the conductor, "the bus leaves in ten minutes, but it takes twice as long as the train. That's because it stops so often. There is also the paddlesteamer that leaves at 2:15 P.M. The steamer takes three times longer than the train."

Can you work out the quickest way to Lakeside?

"I like hexagons," explained Doctor Celia Baker to her two guests. "As you can see I designed *HEX 2* in the shape of a hexagon, which means it has six sides and six corners."

Wendy and Jake agreed that hexagons looked good.

"I like the way hexagons fit together," elaborated Doctor Baker. "Bees build their hives in hexagons. Did you know that? And snowflakes always crystallize as hexagons. Never with five or seven sides, but always with six. Isn't that interesting?"

Doctor Baker pointed at a blue space station nearby. "That one was designed by Professor Pentus. He prefers pentagons. Sometimes our spare parts get mixed up. Oh no, I can see it has happened again; they have sent us five-sided frames. What's the matter with these people, can't they count? I'll have to send them all back and order new ones."

"Wait," said Wendy. "Not all of the frames are wrong. I can see some hexagons among them."

Wendy was correct. But how many of the frames were right and how many were wrong?

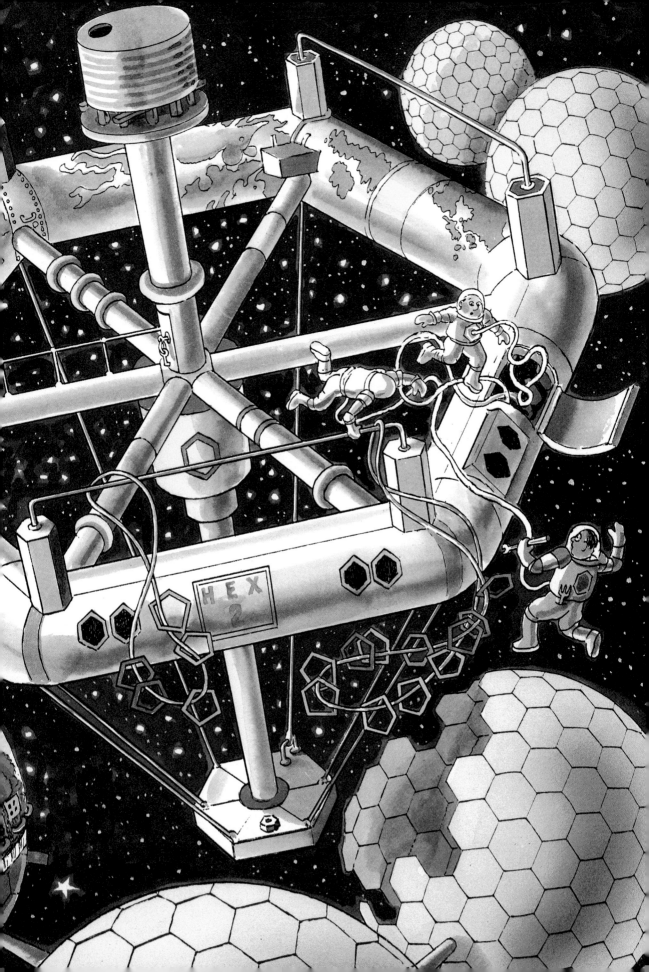

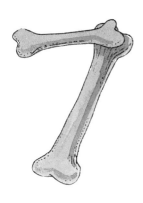

7

Kirstin and Eugene were helping Professor Gruber in the construction of the museum's new dinosaur models. It was very interesting work, although a bit scary at times. The models looked so lifelike! They were cleaning up when Eugene called out, "Oh no, here are three parts left over. Professor Gruber is going to inspect our work in a minute. We'd better find out where these parts belong!" "Don't worry," said Kirstin, "that won't take us long."

Would you find it just as easy?

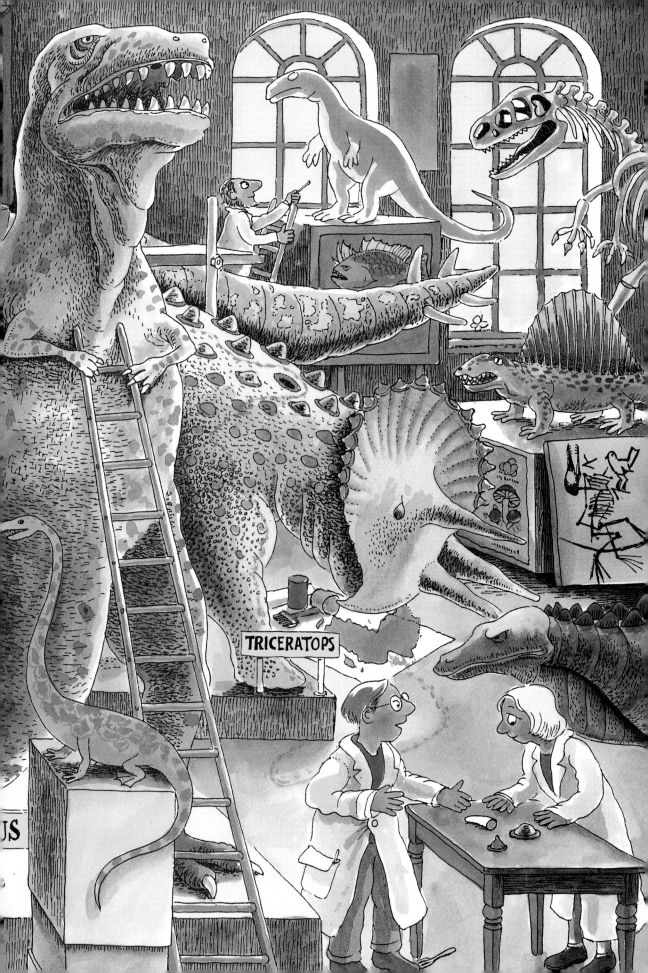

Lani and Robert were trying to deliver an important letter to Santa Claus. To their dismay they suddenly saw themselves surrounded by lots of men in red.

"There can be only one real Santa Claus," whispered Lani. "The others must be his helpers."

"Or fakes," added Robert. "Let's try and spot the fakes. The real Santa Claus would never smoke. And he wouldn't wear anything but black boots. He wouldn't wear sunglasses either, or earrings, or belt buckles with skulls. And he wouldn't read financial papers. He can't be skinny and his cap must be reasonably floppy..."

"You are right," agreed Lani. "That leaves only one of them who could be real."

Can you spot him too?

Building a tree house can be a lot of fun - but not when you're in a wheelchair. Unable to get up the ladder, Danny did what he could to help from the ground by calling out advice and warnings such as: "The window's crooked!" or "A flying saucer's coming!"

Danny was right. A strange spacecraft slowly descended on the backyard, a ladder was dropped and two purple creatures climbed out. Their names were Clax and Dax. Clax said aloud, "Greetings, your majesty."

Danny interrupted him, "Just a moment. My name is actually Danny Myers. How come you speak English? And do you *really* have eyes all around your head?"

"We took a correspondence course," explained Dax. "And yes, we do have six eyes. So we don't need rear view mirrors. However, it makes our glasses rather expensive. And that is the reason for our visit. Clax dropped his glasses and he wants to write a letter home. Have you seen a pair of hexagonal glasses?"

"A pair?" laughed Danny. "Shouldn't you call it a *ring* of glasses? As a matter of fact I've been looking at it all morning and wondering what it was!"

Can you see it too?

"What are those kids doing here?" bellowed Matt, the chief engineer of the *Majeo* team. "Is this a secret project or not? Get them out of here!"

"Oh, please sir," begged Patrick. "I only want to make a quick sketch of your secret plane and Kate here wants to jot down a few technical details. We're not spies or anything. It's for our school magazine." Matt hesitated, then said, "Well, in that case, go ahead. Just don't ask us about our propulsion system."

"Why not? What sort of propulsion system do you use?" asked Kate.

"Well," whispered Matt, "the plane is powered by two electrical motors. The electricity comes from a combination of lightweight batteries and solar cells."

"Marvelous!" exclaimed Kate. "I guess that means no pollution, and it must be silent and cheap to run. But tell me, why do you call the plane *Majeo*?"

"I'm sorry," said Matt, "but I cannot tell you. It is, after all, a secret project, and I'm no blabbermouth. But don't look so sad. It's not so hard to work out why, and if you do I'll give you a ride as the first passengers."

Yes, Patrick and Kate found it easy and they were looking forward to their first flight in the Majeo.

What an incredibly interesting tomb they had found! Although grave robbers must have been here before and left it in a mess, it was still full of mysterious things.

The expedition leader P. Stonnell was especially excited.

"Look at this!" she called from the stairs. "If only this tablet were complete. I believe that the symbol on it is of special significance. Before you do anything else, please help me find the rest of the tablet."

The other parts are still somewhere in the tomb.

Can you find them?

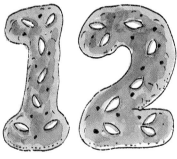

Harley and Elliot lost their way in the forest. Suddenly they came upon a house - a very unusual house made of gingerbread and icing sugar. Who else but a witch would make a house like that? And there she was, standing in the doorway and rubbing her hands together.

"Come on, dear boys, don't be shy," she said, "help yourselves to my lovely sweets."

"No thanks," said Harley. "We didn't bring our toothbrushes, so we shouldn't have any sweets. But we'd be grateful if you'd show us the way back to town."

"Never mind the town," said the witch, "and never mind your toothbrushes. Whoever heard of boys wanting to brush their teeth? Have some sweets."

"Well, *you* obviously never use a toothbrush," said Harley. "And just look at your teeth now!"

The witch quickly closed her mouth. She knew that her teeth were not the best.

"Oh but I *do* have a toothbrush," she insisted. "And what's more I'll lend it to you. Now where did I put it? Don't you go away now, children."

Harley and Elliot could see the toothbrush - but they were not telling!

It was Sonya's eighth
birthday, and what a party it
was!
Sonya had told all her
friends to come as animals.
Some of them had taken a
lot of trouble with their
costumes and so they made
up for those who hadn't
dressed at all. Sonya had
dressed as a spider. She had
even put paint on her face.
"Am I hot!" said Sonya. "If
this is how spiders feel I'm
glad I'm not a spider. I
must sit down."
"Stay away from the T!"
called Philip.
Sonya stopped.
"Why? Aren't those boxes
safe as seats?"
"Just read what it says on
them," suggested Ena. The
boxes had been her presents.
"It says T," said Sonya. "Yes,
of course, I can read it now!
There's a whole word that
goes around the sides."

*Can you work out what word
is spelled out by the letters?*

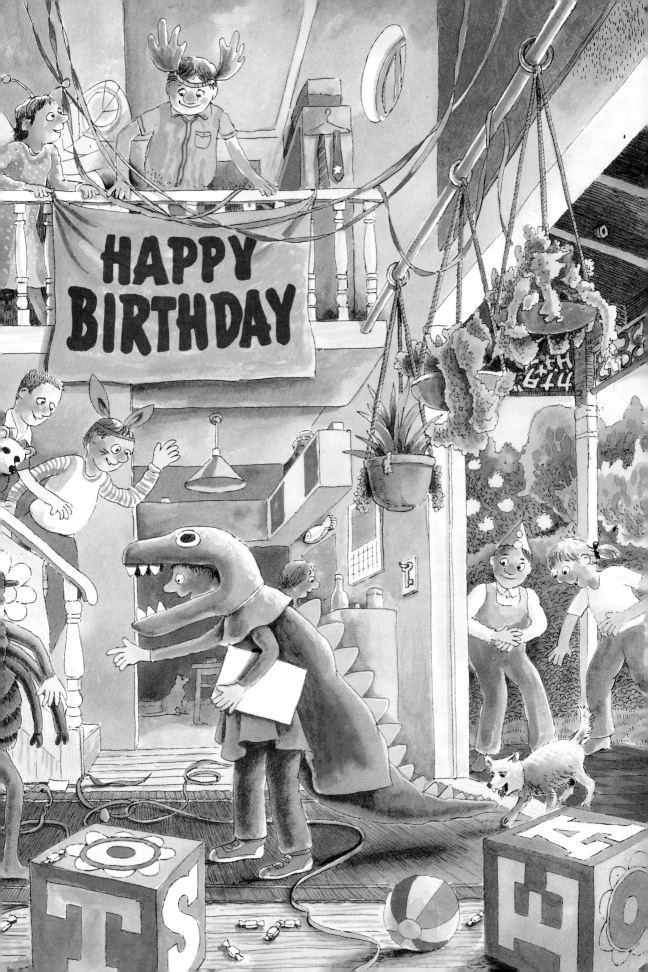

Solutions ... plus a few more surprises!

Vinny found the knife right behind the steering wheel. Quickly he cut the rope and freed Angus.

Together they continued exploring the wreck. They were interested in the name of the ship, but the letters had all fallen off. They could collect the letters, but how would they know in what order to arrange them?

Angus pointed to the screw holes in the hull. By comparing them with the holes in the letters they should be able to work out the name of the ship.

The children discovered the beetle and the butterfly on a tree trunk only a few paces to their right. Sir Pfifferstone took a step toward the tree, then gave a bloodcurdling shriek. He had stepped on a snake and the snake had bitten him.

"Oh no," he groaned. "It's a deadly jumbo mamba! If we don't immediately rub pink snakeweed into the bite I'll be dead within the hour."

"Luckily there's plenty of that around," said Jessie. "How many plants do you need?"

"Three will do," whispered Sir Pfifferstone, growing weaker by the minute. "But wait...don't just take any flower. Use only those that have a black cross in the middle..."

With one stroke of his sword the king's musketeer cut the strings. The balloons *did* rise and *did* wake up Ginger who *did* jump off and *did* drop the weight which *did* make the water overflow and *did* make the wheel turn. But instead of pulling the support from the trap door the string merely slackened. McRob had miscalculated the directions the wheels would turn!

"I arrest you in the name of the king!" said the musketeer. "And while I'm here I'd better check this place out. The queen's crown is missing too and I wouldn't be at all surprised if you had stolen that as well, you rascal!"

"Painter B. Rown, you shall have the crown," said the king, who was also a bit of a poet. "You, dear master Rown, are the only one who managed to get it right. You shall have my lovely daugh..." The king froze in horror - he had just noticed Mr. Rown's feet. "This won't do at all..." he stammered. "My daughter cannot possibly marry a man who goes around with only one sock. In your new position you will have to meet important people such as ambassadors, church leaders, film stars and tennis players. I'd be the laughingstock of the world with a son-in-law like you! I'll give you two minutes to find the other sock or our deal is off."

Let's take the steamer," suggested Anton, "it'll be fun."

"No, our friends are expecting us," Antonio reminded him. "We can take the steamer on the way back. Now let's see - the train, since it is an hour late, will be at Lakeside at 4:00 P.M. The bus, being twice as slow as the train, will take one hour. Since it leaves at 2:08 P.M. it should arrive in Lakeside around 3:08 P.M. And that's much earlier than the steamer. Get your suitcase, we'll take the bus."

Anton and Antonio had the same type of suitcase: blue with a long red stripe. But Anton's suitcase had been mixed up with the luggage from the Eaglestone holiday camp. Luckily they still had a few minutes to find it.

Wendy discovered that the two green frames were hexagons. The other fourteen frames were five-sided, or pentagons.

"It seems that I have to keep my eyes on every little detail," complained Doctor Baker. "The other day two of my workers nearly floated away into space because they didn't attach themselves properly. Come to think of it, I'd better check them now, before it's too late."

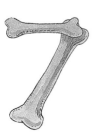

Kirstin put the big white tooth into the mouth of the *Tyrannosaurus* while Eugene discovered that the other parts fitted into the headcrest and the shoulder of *Triceratops*. They finished their job just as Professor Gruber arrived for the inspection.

"Very good, very good," he said, stroking his beard. Then he pondered, "It is true that we don't know what color the dinosaurs were. But I think you went just a little bit overboard with your paint. For instance, why did you paint this green line all over the body of *Triceratops*?"

"I didn't paint a green line," said Kirstin.

Eugene added, "Neither did I."

Well, who did? It was a mystery.

Both Lani and Robert came to the conclusion that the Santa who was sitting closest to the steps was the one properly dressed.

"Excuse me, sir," asked Lani politely, "are you by any chance the real Santa Claus?"

"Sure am, kiddo," said the man.

This made the children immediately suspicious. They thought that the real Santa Claus would never use the word "kiddo."

"If you are the real Santa Claus," said Lani, "then you must be an expert on snow-flakes. Tell me, what's wrong with the snow crystal decorations up there?"

"They look nice to me," said the man - and the children knew that he was an imposter. They knew that real snowflakes always have a certain number of points. The real Santa Claus should know that!

Danny pointed to the tree-fork above where the alien's spectacles had lodged. Clax retrieved them with a stick.

"Thank you, oh King Danny Myers," he said, "and while we're here, may we ask you another favor? What about some fresh water for our goldfish?"

"Help yourself," said Danny. "I'll turn the tap on. Just take the end of the hose and I'll give you all the water you want."

"How kind of you, oh great and generous king," said Clax with a bow, "but, pray tell us - where is the end of the hose?"

Danny laughed.

"You have six eyes in your head and you can't even see the end of the hose?"

Patrick and Kate worked out that the word *Majeo* was made up by the first letter of each team member's name - Matt, Anita, John, Ellen and Olga.

"One more thing puzzles me," said Kate. "Why are the wings painted a different color?"

"Ah, you see," explained Matt, "instead of building two prototypes we built only one plane but with two different wings. If the aircraft flies in a left curve we know that the right wing is faster. If it turns right we know that the left wing is better. Clever, isn't it? Look closely and you'll discover that it's not only the color that's different. There are three other items we have changed."

Ms. Stonnell's assistant found the rest of the tablet in two parts – one under the stairs and the other under the lid of the sarcophagus. As they put the three pieces together, Ms. Stonnell called out, "Just as I thought! A fish!"

"Why is that of special significance?" the assistants wanted to know.

"Because it was the king's symbol. I believe there must be a box in this tomb which contains the scrolls on which the king kept his diary. It should have the same fish symbol on it. We must find it!"

The witch found the toothbrush on the windowsill.

"Here it is!" she called out triumphantly. "Now you'll stay and have some lollies, won't you?"

"Not on your life," said Harley. "Do you really think we'd use your toothbrush? What a disgusting idea. Please tell us the way to town and we'll be off."

The witch stopped smiling. Stamping her feet, she called out, "I want you to stay. If you don't, I'll put a flat-tire-spell on your bikes."

"A flat-tire-spell?" laughed Elliot. "There is no such thing!"

"There is so," said the witch. "All I have to do is to find three animals that rhyme with 'flat,' boil them all up in my cauldron and then make you drink it."

The boys looked around. They didn't really believe in flat-tire-spells and they certainly wouldn't have drunk the liquid. But they thought they might have to save three animals from that crazy old woman!

"The T is part of the word SEAT, isn't it?" said Sonya. "Anybody can see that. But why did you want me to get away from it, Philip? What are you anyway, a lizard? Or a crocodile?"

"I only wanted to avoid confusion," explained Philip, opening the book which he had brought as a present. "You see, there's a spider on each picture and it's always sitting on or near a letter of the alphabet. If you take note of those letters and collect them, in order, from each page you'll find out what sort of animal I am. I'm definitely not a lizard, and I'm not a crocodile either..."
